FAITH
ᴵᴺ ACTION

LOIS E. LUND

The Reading Glass Books
(888) 420-3050
www.readingglassbooks.com
production@readingglassbooks.com

Contents

Acknowledgements

I must say thank you to my husband, Larry, who loves me and takes care of me. Thank you to my nurse, who inspires me to be the best I can be, and inspires me to write. My Doctors, counsellors, pastors, close friends, my friends, my publisher, and colleagues who help me write. I thank my family who have given me hope. I want to thank my Sunday School teacher Helen, who always gave me the benefit of the doubt and loves me. And I thank my God who watches me day and night.

Trips to Iowa

My parents drove to northern Iowa every year for our vacation. That's where we spent two weeks with cousins, aunts and uncles, and most of my relatives. Grandparents, and loved ones. I was a kid in 1960s.

As I know my ancestors from records and experience what I believe is that we were Christian and conservative people. Most of my family on both sides were farmers and grandpa on mom's side was a tenant farmer in the early 1930s.

My cousin was one year younger than me we walked everywhere in town from my aunt's house to grandma's house to the swimming pool in the park and back. We stopped at the little store. I got milk duds and licorice to put under my pillow to eat in bed. My auntie Ruth said we were two little brownies We got tans walking right through the courtyard. In the sun to our grandma's house to my cousin's. She lived in a big white house in a little town. Her house was across from the dried blood plant. They had air pollution for a city block sometimes. I guess air pollution wasn't such a bad thing back then in the 1960's. Anyway farmers families put up with air pollution of some sort or other because of their animals.

This is funny.

My Dad moved away from the farm 6 months after I was born. But we sacrificed closeness with our cousins and grandparents and aunts and uncles. I have often wanted to have a sister, but I have loyal friends now. And our family still sticks together as much as we can by phone. And are together as much as we can be for the holidays.

Grandma greeted me at the door she would hold my face and kiss my cheek and said, "Much success to you." She smiled and clapped her hands. Grandpa sat in his great chair with his suit on in front of the window and watched for squirrels and birds and people walking by. Grandpa had cancer I think he was 86. They had such a big family. They had seven children I think they saw some every day. We sat down to eat at the big "Oak" table and had roast beef and peaches and once rutabagas plus the scrumptious grandma's brown bread which was eaten with butter and honey and milk. ummmm. Where ever we went to visit as a family we had a delicious meal with our family. We said grace in our prayer for the blessing of food. We played the old pump organ so loud. Also there was an old fashioned cylinder RCA record player, and the "view finder" apparatus to see pictures of men in their tall hats and women in their big hoop skirts a ferry boat. You open a Christmas candy can and green snake comes out!

Iowa was farmland. There were fields of corn, soy beans and straw and alfalfa to feed this country and other countries too. There were hay fields to feed the animals and straw to for bedding for the animals in cold weather in their barns.

Usually farmer's wives had a garden tomatoes, carrots, green beans to pick and snap for canning, sweet corn and peas, radishes, loose leaf lettuce too, strawberries, too rhubarb, gooseberries apples, broccoli, and yes onions too. The good earth was yielding table food. All of these great foods. Had to be washed canned or frozen to preserve these.

Grandpa Gilbert had three farms. He bought some land when it was cheap in the early 1940s He had several sons to work the farms. My dad, Uncle John, and Uncle Lawrence, Uncle Alan, Uncle Grant. They had seven children.

My dad moved away from the farm, with his family four kids. He moved out of Iowa to a promising job waiting for him in Indiana in Mitchell county. My little brother was born there so there were five of us kids. Dad's promising job fell through. There weren't any jobs except for Kokomo 10 miles east of Greentown where Dad found a good job in Stellite Factory a Union Carbide Company. He worked another part time job. Francis Maple aluminum siding and windows and doors company was his part time job. Dad did a good job there. He liked the Maple family. Dad didn't see us kids very much. He had to work. Dad served our country in the Coast Guard. He said they took German soldiers My brothers and I agree our parents depended on God for their lives.

Back home in Indiana

My Mother got up in the morning in summer while it was still cool and put on her one pair of pants to hoe and plant and go out in her garden. One year it was on the south pasture. Another year her gardening was in the north pasture. I wanted to help so I used the Rotor Tiller to get the grass and weeds out of the garden. Then we'd pick green beans and tomatoes. We planted potatoes eyes I know what it is to dig new potatoes and wash them. They're easy to keep. Mom did a lot of canning tomatoes, and pears from the pear tree. She had a little crab apple tree for pies. There was rhubarb growing freely back at the neighbor's fence. Mom made strawberry/rhubarb pie. There were little elderberries along the fence on the east fence. She made jam out of those. There was sweet corn on the cob. On Sundays Dad would pick sweet corn for Sunday dinner. I set the table for most dinners I liked to get Kentucky Fried chicken. I loved that for Sunday dinner.

Mom planted sunflower seeds. Big ol' sunflowers a row of them brown and yellow. I took a picture of mom in her dress standing by them. In front of the Garden. I can see it with mom standing there in her pretty dress. Mom was a big woman like me. We have so much energy. She went to exercise classes to lose weight. Dad gave her aluminum siding on the house. Mother went to teacher's College, in her home state, Iowa and taught school in a one room school for nine years. She used flannel graph figures on an easel to tell us Bible stories in Sunday School. It wasn't very fancy nor were there pictures on the wall. It was in the basement of a very old church. A Wesleyan Methodist Church. We learned Stories from the Bible mom used flannel graph on an easel

4

to bring bible stories and missionary stories to life. I was with Mom a lot. She taught missionary stories and she taught Old Testament familiar stories. And she taught Good News Club in our home. She was in her field of expertise. Some times Mother taught in our elementary school to help out. When a teacher had to be away. I remember her teaching my elementary class once. Teaching was her forte. She did that best. But she was so concerned for those who were less fortunate than we. She took in two foster kids, Steven and Stacy. When is was young.

Growing up in Indiana the beautiful Queen Ann's Lace plant along the roadsides. It's a wonder of nature. It's a long stemmed plant growing wild and free along the roadsides in middle America.

This Indiana is where I grew up. The flower blooms out just like a white crochet piece. My Grandma taught me how to crochet. I made some doilies. At home in Indiana I mowed the yard sometimes. I watched TV. I ironed. I made chile. I refinished my bedroom furniture in antiquing. Made a pair of white pants with cuffs. In the garage I watched our white kitty give birth to some little babies in a box with cloth. We had a beagle dog who had babies. I played with them. She loved Mom. She would wiggle her tail and smile at Mom. In the summer when I was in Jr. high I had music lessons with my band director.

There is still something about Indiana that I love. Overcast days. In the fall my hair would shine dark brown. In Jr. High I got up one morning and found a new hairdo, it lay just where I brushed it front to back and it would part on the side. That was my interest in my hair do or style. I let my bangs grow out and the sides grew out too and when I went to the fair I had a Beatles hairstyle.

I had trauma when I was growing up. I was a little ornery. I didn't think I would grow up to be bipolar. I have learned that I have to cope with it. I can't do it without my support system. I was pretty depressed at eighteen. My dad thought I had a problem so did mom but I was never checked until I joined the U.S. Navy in 1975. I was 24. I have pills now. I have coped with this for 40 years.

I'm bipolar. We who have this disability are the most vulnerable to mishaps. They are prey to those who are full of mischief. Misunderstood in an over more that It's better now that I take an anxiety pill I am happier now that I do.

The old hymn says, "There is no other argument there is no other plea but Jesus died upon that cross and that He died for me." That's enough to know to keep you going.

I practiced my trumpet every day at home for a half hour. I liked playing it and I was good. I began playing it in fifth grade. We started music with flute phones. And I had piano lessons. I didn't like piano too many keys. There was one note at a time with trumpet. That was my instrument. I played my trumpet in church. I learned so many hymns and other Christian music which is the best music ever written, contemporary as well speaks to hearts. It was such a blessing to me and a challenge to learn. Utube is gospel music.

Mom bought me two new trumpets a Conn one in my Jr. high years and a Bach trumpet in high school I liked trumpet. It was a challenge and I could do it. I had four brothers. So I felt comfortable playing sports with the boys in elementary school. So it was music and sports that took up most of my time.

In school our stage band played at basketball games and we played "CHARGE" and other songs. One was "I'll Be Around." It was from the big band era. I had a solo part in that song.

Our marching band played at our home football games. Our uniforms were green wool and we had on fuzzy white five gallon hats. Mom really smiled in church when I played my trumpet. She enjoyed that so much.

We went to the "Indy" 500 festivities in Indianapolis, Indiana. That was a two and a half mile race track a real work out for anybody on foot; and we played our instruments too; songs that we had learned in the band room at school. Our band director gave us some nice proud memories while he was our band director. He also invited "Doc"

Severinsen from Johney Carson's Tonight's Show to play Bugler's Holiday in a trumpet trio with myself and the other trumpet player next to me and the whole concert band in high school. Our band director gave us kids so many good opportunities. He even gave music lessons in the summer after school was out.

After high school I did some babysitting. Then I got a waitress job in a diner in Kokomo Indiana. I made toast and buttered it too. Didn't have a plan for my future I didn't think much about it Mom talked to me about college I worked at two restaurants and a busy burger joint. Mom and me would drive to my job, night shift, and she would go to her job then she'd pick me up and we'd go home in the morning. We both worked nights.

It was time for me to go to College. Then I packed up and Mom and Dad dropped me off at school at Tennessee Temple College. She had a great vacation time. I went to the school office then to registration lines. It was pretty cut out for me I didn't have a job. Didn't think much about working but mom did mention getting a job at college, I couldn't see myself working with some of those big girls like one who was so big and strong but she was having a good time.

I should have got a job too then it would have been better for me and help mom too I would have been good if I had a job. I ran myself "ragged" on that girl's basketball team. Working would have been better I could really help out to my advantage I was 19. Then when I was twenty I would be established an actually earning money at a real job. My other two jobs back home were the pits. It would have been better to find a good employer and Christian people to work for. Somewhere I missed it. My life was with myself with no future plans. I made it through the year in college in Tennessee, majored in music. Wrote my first poem, took speech class. Speech was difficult for me but I'm glad I took it.

I moved to Iowa where my roots were. I was born in Iowa after I was finished with college I worked at a gas station. I pumped gas and checked oil dipsticks. Rang up sales, cleaned windows I was available for work. Mr. Elliott Was a very nice man to hired me. He helped me buy four new tires at a discount. I didn't know I needed them. He used to love to eat popcorn at home. He taught me to balance a wheel with lead weights. I rang up some sales, but I didn't know how to keep his books. Another girl did that.

I worked at Road heaver Publishing Company coallating books for a few months while I was still in college. Next I got a job at the International Harvester Store in town in Iowa. I didn't make enough money to heat grandma's house and buy food too. The Fuel was outrageous. $99.00 a month. My aunt and uncle asked me if need money for the winter heating bill. Of course I said, "No I had enough." Well I had to pinch at the grocery store.

I also painted some on Mr. Lund's farm where my boyfriend lived. And I painted some on Helen' s house. I also painted on Uncle John's barn.

I hoed button weeds for cash money that was the best job. I learned to love cold tea there. I also dug a field with a tractor to get the dirt ready for planting. I used a good old tractor with an attached digger for my friend's dad.

I was a disappointment to my other grandma. She told me I couldn't stay with her any more. Well, I was being a problem. We were kids, my little brother and I. He passed away a couple months ago. David, my oldest brother sent his journal entries and letters. I miss him. He was very busy. He was a percussionist. He studied percussion instruments and music at Indiana University. He knew all the percussion instruments and played in orchestras, bands and taught private lessons. He always did the best he could I miss him. I would have called him more often. He had a lot of acquaintances. I was his sister. We used to play together outside. He played the drums and I practiced my trumpet for a half hour every day. We watched Saturday morning TV. And played imaginary fun outside in Indiana. Back home in Indiana my little brother and I play-n acted television shows on Saturday morning. It's true all of them were westerns .When you were shot you closed your eyes for 30 seconds. Tarzan of the jungle was my favorite show on Saturday mornings.

New Story

It was horrendous day! One Saturday afternoon it rained, it was a monsoon, lightning and thunder and I was out in it with an umbrella on foot with my friend. I wish my husband had not taken me there. I had a good umbrella. We took the bus to the Wal-Mart area. Didn't want to go to Wal Mart!

There is a day you will see him, Jesus in heaven. Some day he will come back and take us to heaven with him. All have sinned and come short of the glory of God. You need to prepare for your future. Every day will live forever in one place or another. Our belief is that there are two places to live continually heaven is the place see Jesus and the prophets of old and our ancestors who believed.

You don't want to go to the other place. Please hear what I say. The Bible backs me up. There is an eternal separation from the good forever called the bad place or as we read in the Bible; hell below. You are lost and need to be saved. Admit that you're a sinner and you need Jesus to wash your sins away. He will and you get promises, like he'll never leave you or forsake you. No one can take that away from you. You will go to heaven when your time on earth is over.

My mother is there, my dad too. My grandparents. And aunts and uncles. But most of all there will be a huge sigh of relief for me. Then I won't be wanting to be there so much, but I have a job to do as an author. Now I will be busy and happy. Up there in heaven I will be changed. That's what God promises in his Bible. But until then I must be busy in his work. I'm an author. I've written three books. I'm writing book four.

On this earth, there are signs and changes in the weather. America has faced snow storms, floods. Fires, inclement weather more than ever. Tsunames and earthquakes in other countries, such as now. Massive devastation we have seen this year here in America, how tragic.

Hurricane "Matthew" came to Orlando, FL we survived even without electricity one day. To cope with my disability. I take pills and I'm not so groggy any more. "Matthew" we didn't have electricity but we had water. There were leaves on the street. I didn't' go out of the house except for church and I have milk. There were leaves on out street our big tree took the wind but it stayed intact this time. Hurricane.

"Charlie was worse than Matthew."

For the word of God is quick.

And sharper than any two edged sword,

Piercing even to the dividing asunder of the joints and marrow And a discerner of the thoughts and intents of the heart.

Marilyn taught music to high school kids and She had a friend who taught too. Both of these were mothers who had daughters who were cheerleaders, both of them. Marilyn played the piano in church. She was teaching the difference of classical music to high school kids to rock and roll and what a bad influence rock and roll was to the kids in her class. One of the boys had two restless feet that wouldn't stay still. She didn't think he paid any attention in class. This boy brought in good music to class one day and it surprised her. Her students learned. She left the class room for a minute or two one day and they put stardust; glitter in her purse. She didn't go back. She didn't really want to be a teacher. She played the piano for the offertory at church she didn't stop, She played the whole piece and she got a standing ovation. Her mom was there too.

"HAY, YOU!"

STRAW IS CHEAPER, GRASS IS FREE.

BUY A FARM AND GET ALL THREE!!!

Tom and Mary Witt

Marilyn played the piano one evening. She taught at Orlando, Christian School Powers Drive. Her kids sold soda cans to pay for the hand bells they played for Christmas programs and all year through. She left her mark there too.

Marilyn has met the Lone Ranger twice. She also wrote her own version of her book, "The Lone Ranger."

Marilyn taught music to high school kids and She had a friend who taught too. Both of these were mothers who had daughters who were cheerleaders. Marilyn played the piano in church. She was teaching the difference of classical music to high school kids to rock and roll and what a bad influence rock and roll was to kids. One of the boys had two restless feet that wouldn't stay still. She didn't think he paid any attention in class. This boy brought in good classical music to class one day and it surprised her.

Her students learned. She left the class room for a minute or two one day and they put stardust; glitter in her purse. And she didn't go back. She didn't really want to be a teacher. On another occasion, she played the organ for the offertory one day and she didn't stop. She played the whole piece and she got a standing ovation. Her mom was there too. She had fun filled times in Christian college Radio and TV Production major.

Marilyn played the piano one evening. Marilyn is gifted. Marilyn remembers. I went to kindergarten and christian school in first grade. The experience lasted one year. The only thing I learned was I would never again go to school on a school bus.

Second grade was at a public school in a town I lived in on and off. We moved a lot. No, My father wasn't in the military. In third grade, I went to a small country school in a small country town.

That was the year I nearly died of a kidney infection. Our family doctor was forty miles away. When my parents told him my symptoms and that another in town had died. My Dr. said, "Get her down here NOW!"

My parents wrapped me in a blanket and put me in the back seat of a Plymouth Coupe. When we reached the doctor's office, my father took me into the building where his office was . He rang the doorbell to let the doctor know we were there. The nurse admitted us and went into the treatment room. She prepared for me giving me a shot of one hundred CCs of penicillin while I screamed as if I was dying.

I went to a school in a Larger city in farm country. Finally we settled in Ferndale, Michigan, where I finished my required education. Instead of going to college, I managed to get a good jobs close to my home. The first one was at a large department store in down town Detroit. I was a clerk in the office of the upscale hats for a year. The next job was closer to home. It was a job in a large bank chain and stayed there about three years. Then I decided to learn key punch for cards to be printed out. After I learned how to key punch, I stayed in the computer room about six months. But because of my work at the bank I was asked to go to accounts receivable. I didn't want to go but it was more money and better hours. I got a job in a factory that made industrial ovens. I stayed there about three months.

I applied for a job at Standard Oil. I was closer to home and in a better area. I stayed at Standard Oil until it I decided to go to college. By this time I was twenty two years old. My first semester started in January instead of September. My first dorm was with teenagers. In September, I was moved to a dorm for girls over twenty and "The dorm Mother, dubbed our home. "The dorm of unclaimed blessings." Jennie was Amish and had reddish blond hair. We all loved her. Back in January, I had auditioned for Classic Players, a group of upper class men and faculty who put on a Shakespeare play. I was not chosen.

However all was not in vain. As I was walking back to my "blessings dorm." A female teacher accosted me, "I've been looking all over campus for you!" Well, I thought, what ever does she want from me. She came right to the point. "I want you to be in vespers. She said. If you'll come to my office, I'll tell you what you'll need." So I went with her to her office. "First, you'll need a green gown. She handed me a piece of paper. I had four verses about Christmas. The last verse was mine. Memorize it, she told me. She went on to tell me when the rehearsal would be, etc. Before I left her office, She told me that she was at the auditions for Classic Players. She told me they liked my voice. Well, I did not make Classic players, but being in vespers was saying, "You have arrived, girl!" Only upperclassmen were chosen to be on vespers. I was still a freshman. The irony of this was, I was subbing for the darling of the Speech Department; She had an appointment elsewhere.

To most people a missionary is someone who leaves their home town go into a jungle or into a foreign country. In most cases that's true. However you can be a missionary In your town. I was barely out of high school when I was asked one day go down town to a Salvation Army Mission. My parents allowed me to go with two men from our church. I Loved it , I played the piano. Jim Whitford was known by me and my father. One night at Harvard Street Mission Jim and his friend went upstairs to pray for the service the men prayed and when they finished Jim said my name. I knew he wanted me to pray for the service. I did and while I prayed I experienced a warm sensation.

Well, my missions were over when I left for college. But before I left a Salvation Army Sargent paid me a compliment. "I see you come here with different groups. To which one do you belong?"

"None," I replied. "Well, aren't you a missionary?" I thanked him and I could have said I'm the only person they could get to come down to Skid Row and play the piano. I miss those days.

After all was said and done, I was playing the piano at five missions. Two Salvation Army Missions, The Detroit Rescue Mission, Howard Street Mission and New life mission.

Thank you Marilyn for that great story.

I met Doc Severinsen and played the "Bugler's Holiday for Trumpets" with my other trumpet player in high school concert band. We had a show for the musicians in Howard County. "Doc" was the band leader on the Johnny Carson tonight show. Our Band director brought good memories for us in 1969 the year I was a senior.

My brother built his racer in Indiana mid Summer in the city there was the Soap Box Derby for the guys. He built it with wood and the mesh plastic cover. He painted it silver. Their tires and 2 axles and steering wheel were given to them. He spun those wheels with a towel to break them in for speed. It was on Markham Street in Kokomo, Indiana. The boys in the Soap Box Derby who won in their towns the fastest Derby winners went to Boys scout camp in Akron Ohio. The Parents went to banquets. The boys voted to see the men on Bonanza TV show. Lorne Greene, Hoss Cartwright and Michael Landon meeting the stars. They treated the parents with a Hotel Room. Funny, I didn't even remember that my parents were gone.

The church of Azalea Park, Orlando had the faithful members Tom and Mary. Tom had a lung collapse. His parents came down from Virginia to see him. That same morning the ladies had a prayer Meeting and prayed for Tom. He was perfectly healed. At the Drs. office he said go home Tom there is nothing wrong with your lungs.

Tom and Mary have worked and given most of their time to keep our church going. They drive 40 miles one way to church. They have a beautiful big black car with a wheelchair carrier for Mary. She has to keep oxygen on most of the time. She does the church secretarial work and helps keep track of the budget, income, and expenses.

Mary gave birth to her daughter, Crystal, but she had something wrong there. The Dr. said it was a tumor. Mary knew it couldn't be another baby, so Mary asked for anointing oil and prayer at church and asked God to heal her. Well, he certainly did. The tumor left and that's another blessing from God in heaven.

Clifford, their son's lung collapsed after 5 surgeries. The Dr. let him go. Mary and Tom Have done the custodial and secretarial and upkeep of the building and paid the bills with the offering.

Cathy had a 12 month old baby in her car. Cathy had been having heart trouble. She was on Goldenrod Road and Curry Ford Road. She was at a stop light. When the light changed. She just sat there. She couldn't go. And just as she didn't go a car turned in front of her. She wasn't hurt at all.

I was in school, first chair trumpet in band. Mother bought me a new trumpet. A Conn one in my Jr. high years and a Bach trumpet in high school. I liked trumpet. It was a challenge and I could do it. I had four brothers. So I felt comfortable playing sports with the boys in elementary school. So it was music and sports that took up most of my time.

I practiced my trumpet every day at home for a half hour. I liked playing it and I was good. I began playing it in fifth grade. We started music with flute phones. And I had piano lessons. I didn't like piano, too many keys.

To most people a missionary is someone who leaves their home town to go into a jungle or a foreign country. In most instances that's true. However, you can be a missionary in your town.

I was barely out of high school when I was asked one day to go down town to a Salvation Mission Army.

One night, when the front door opened and Jim Whitford came in. I shrieked! I forgot what day it was.. I got out of my chair where I was munching on pistachios and I made haste to my bedroom. I took off my duster and put on the clothes I was wearing that day. I brushed my hair and put on some lipstick. I brushed my teeth.

And went into the living room. I said, "Let's go." "All ready?" The men asked. They couldn't believe I changed in about five minutes.

My parents allowed me to go with two men from our church.. I loved it. Jim Whitford was known by me and my father. One night at Harverd Street Mission.

Jim and his friend and me went upstairs to pray for the service. The men prayed and when they finished Jim said my name. I knew he wanted me to pray for the service. I experienced a warm sensation.

Marilyn was very talented and played the piano well too.. We went to her house and I took my trumpet and we loved playing the old Hymns and happy Christian music.

I LOVED EVERY MINUTE OF BEING A HOME TOWN MISSIONARY.

It is beautiful to see a parent support a Down Syndrome Child and help them participate in trips to the beauty parlor or restaurant and go to church. I saw one of those children going to the beauty school with her mother, to a school, or to the store or restaurant. I am doing my best to write about what I've been through. You feel like who trusts anybody now. There is a point when you must trust somebody bigger than you or me. Maybe they can't read. Some are war veterans in need. There is always someone who will help. Let's hope! I don't like to hear someone say to someone who wants to jump off a tall building or a bridge, and say go ahead and jump. In California, there is a man who makes it his calling to help people who are so destitute that they will want to jump off the bridge. You just don't know about people. Maybe they are in pain. Or Post Traumatic, Stress, Syndrome from war or rape, or personal catastrophe. They need a close friend or counselor.

Queen Ann's Lace

I grew up in Indiana. Four seasons I miss them. I loved the snow. Sometimes you had to be very careful in the snow and ice. There was the beautiful Queen Ann's Lace plant along the roadsides. It's a wonder of nature. It's a long stemmed plant growing wild and free along the roadsides in middle AMERICA. It has a lacey embroidered look bloom.

There is still something about Indiana that I love. Overcast days. In the fall my hair would shine. In Florida there is a plant that is yucky without rain. When it thrives it is sheen lavender. I don't know it's name it is so delicate.

There is a plant in Florida is the blue blossoms that you can grow in a favorite spot like around a mailbox. It seems to last a long time. Sometimes In school our stage band played at basketball games. Our marching band was a real work out for anybody on foot besides playing an instrument. I had no future plans. So mom talked to me and we decided I would go to college in Tennessee. Christian College. I made it through the year. And wrote my first poem there and took speech class. I liked my trumpet teacher. He was so funny.

He played an oil funnel like he played his trumpet. He played "Stars and Stripes" on it. It was really impressive and funny! He led the brass choir and I was in it. I lived in a dormitory for women and had a few friends. I woke up every day dressed have breakfast and go to my first class. I went to College for 1 1/2 years. Both religious colleges. Got pretty good grades. I was losing my independence. I could not do anything. I needed Mom.

In Florida it will rain a lot. And it rained today. Today going to rain I Don't think it's at all. According to my weather report it will be sunny all day. Had just a teeny bit of rain. In Junior High school our stage band played at basketball games. Our marching band played for football games it was a real work out for anybody on foot besides playing an instrument.

In my heart I had no future plans after high school. I worked two places after high school. Mom and I worked nights. She was an admissions's clerk. So mom talked to me and we decided I would go to college in Tennessee Temple College.

Christian College. I made it through the year. And wrote my first poem there and took speech class. I liked my trumpet teacher.

The words of God are telling us that faith is the substance of things hoped for; the evidence of things not seen. Through faith we understand that the worlds were framed by the words of God so that things which are seen were made of things which do not appear. This scripture is good because it tells us about faith and how real it is. It's pure logic. God knows what all things are made of. And all things are made of things that we can't see with the naked eye. There are cells. finely tuned body tissue and the human body is a miracle of God's creation. Everything that was made, was made by God himself.

John 3:16 says those who believe in Jesus hould not perish but Have Everlasting life, that is eternal life in heaven.

There are other remedies that we help those two percent of our population There are other remedies that we. The mind is a terrible thing to waste is so true. I used to watch TV commercials. Our bipolar. schizophrenic, emotionally battered friends and some go to into a dark hole that takes time to get out of. Depression is a terrible sickness. It's a condition that is treatable.

They must be saved by our all powerful mighty God We need prayer and intervention and love for these people. They become so lost in their illness just terribly sick at heart and soul, depressed the straight word of God..... The Bible is truth. Holistic healing is a method of teaching healing which is in this book for those who need a refresher in mental and emotional strength which is more detailed and written comprehensively. I read about holistic healing about a year ago.

I was at my worst when I was raped at a mental facility. I didn't know how to protect myself or get counseling after that. I was a basket case. I have spoken to my nurse about that and also a lady at church. Methods of recovery are also written in a book called Genuine Recovery. This book is larger and much more detailed than my book. I also have written another book called MIND. PAIN. FEELING. HEALING. It very helpful for those who have a chemical imbalance or mental problem.

It is filled with truths about we who are in bondage and feel lost at times. I guess we all do at times. Here is what I'm trying to say to you. Although you may not want to read your Bible. Many have learned to read and we owe so much of our good health to medical science. But without faith it is hard to treat. God wants us all to have faith in him. Just trust Him to take care of us.

May God bless those who want to be friends with those who have chemical imbalances. We need the fellowship with others. I'm thankful for that I took my evening pills I'll be sleeping in a little while. My nurse took that day off. She loves her days off. She does a lot of driving while she's working too. So does my husband. He drives a lot too. I don't know when He'll be home.

Clergy have helped so much. Marriage counselors, those with experience and knowledge, professionals, Those who are aware of these maladies. It took me 30 long years to find my medicine; years to know myself with prayers. Letting others know how I feel and their prayers help me keep me going on. They just said, "Take your pills." We must take our medication. Must endure the fight to take back our lives. With the help and love and caring of our elite group of helpers. Nurses, Doctors, Medical research, friends, prayer warriors Pastors, Reverends.

I must know I'm never alone my church family and my husband and my family know I've have hard times. But do I pray for them and hold them up before God too. We all have problems. I need to learn about others and respect them too.

I spent 3 months of my life searching in my mind for the answer to any problem or question I had. I don't think I wasted those three months. I wanted to know the meaning of life. I would think about any angle I could but I found out that everything goes in a cycle of truth and untruths. That God has the basic truth in every thought or action if we're tuned in I now have to know how to love as I should and pray for them and those causes I support.

EVERY GOOD THING AND EVERY PERFECT THING COMES FROM GOD.

I wanted to be with mother. I wanted her to console me. I wanted her to talk to me but I never really knew what that was like. When she became disappointed with me she let me know. But she really didn't know me. The year I went home to see my Mother. God took her from us in a senseless car wreck. Two guys in speeding car drunk or on drugs. Out of control they slammed into my Mother broadside. The crash tore the whole front end off the car. My sister in law called the house. She said, "Come right over to the hospital where mom worked. She was in a bad car accident, drive sensible." So I told my brother and we drove over there probably in twenty minutes. Mom passed away in the emergency room at the hospital where she worked. I could not cry, I was numb. I wanted to see her.

I was devastated. I had only been home a month to see mom. I should have gone with her to the church but I didn't think I was any good to her. I very well could have been with her. I was almost totally lost. I could have been the car with mom.

I was too depressed to go with her. Nobody had talked to me. I just called a line on the phone. It helped. I didn't know what to do. I could have prayed. I just did a few minutes ago. Sometimes things go so wrong, praying is the only answer. Because God hears you. After some recuperation Dad told me about a job with a chicken restaurant. I was washing pans and dishes. The owner's wife showed me how she made baked beans. I moved to Iowa where my Grandma and Aunt lived. My folks started in Iowa. I was looking for my roots. My college friends were not enough for me. And it was a big expense to go to college. If I had been smart enough I should have tried singing with a musical guy who was looking for somebody to sing with him. I could have I was just too insecure. I should have taken him up on that. It would have been fun. I was scared to do anything like that. But it would have been so easy and fun now as I look back. I know how to sing harmony. But I never thought of myself as a singer. Just in church. I was devastated after mom passed away. Had no plans and nobody I knew and my oldest brother took it hard. I stayed at their place one night. I was a student I didn't ask for asked for advice. I didn't know how. I didn't know to trust anybody's advice. I took up my trumpet and played with the concert band in Kokomo in the auditorium. There was a young lady who played solo trumpet with the orchestra. That was remarkable. One time my Dad brought a lady to the concert and I met them afterwards. That was so good for dad.

But I wasn't happy. It was a case of depression and undiagnosed prohibitive mental problems. I was carrying a big load of doubt and loneliness I didn't know anything about what I should do. In elementary school I was *Gooey* my friends called me in elementary school. it was a play on words with my first and last names. I didn't mind it. My Mother went to the school to complain. I never thought anything bad about that nickname. They took my first name. Looey and attached my last name to it. Gilbert and attached the first letter of my last name G and made Gooey out of it. It was OK. With me. I loved recess.

The words of God are telling us that faith is the substance of things hoped for; the evidence of things not seen. Through faith we understand that the worlds were framed by the words of God so that things which are seen are made of things which do not appear. This scripture the words of God are telling us that faith is the substance of things hoped for; the evidence of things not seen. Through faith we understand that the worlds were framed by the words of God so that things which are seen were made of things which do not appear. This scripture is good because it tells us about faith and how real it is. It's pure logic. God knows what all things are made of And all things are made of things that we can't see with the naked eye. There are intricut body tissue and the human body is a miracle of God's creation. Everything that was made, was made by God himself. That who ever believes in Him should have everlasting life.

Our enemy is the one that hates God. He is the Devil. He wants to harm you any way he can. Don't let him!

The victims of mental diseases and emotional trauma and injury they wandered about. With no sense or direction. There are powers of darkness, of which the whole world knows of evil and good, unless they are blinded from the truth some how. Our Bible is our study book to know God and that He sent his son for our salvation. When there is a great trouble inside a that person needs to hear the good news that there is that there was a man on earth who had the power to overcome all that. That's the reason I write this to help you. I can read my Bible and go to church just as anybody can.

Jesus, while he was here brought back to life some who were dead. He helped those who asked for help. All the libraries couldn't hold all the books that would be written with the things Jesus did in his work here on earth.

Mary and Martha were sisters. They were so sad Jesus hadn't been there when their friend Lasarus had died. Jesus knew them too and he was moved to tears by their loss. He went to Lasarus tomb and called him to rise. Well, Lasarus came out of the tomb in his bandages and it was a very famous miracle and the non -believers in Jesus became very angry at the power Jesus showed.

God's still in charge and we can confess our sins and he will accept you just as you are and you can ask Him anything.

Noah's story. I love this story. You will see how good this story is. It had not rained on the earth before. God told Noah of Genesis to build an ark with all the instructions. His family helped him. Nobody had seen rain before. God's plan was to make it rain for 40 days and nights upon the earth. Everything drown upon the earth even those who made fun of him. This is a wonder of the world. Noah took a lot of ridicule and he had to ignore it. Have you ever done anything by sheer faith? Of course you have. God Gave Noah the dimensions and he built a big boat in the sandy desert. He used tar to pitch the wood to keep it from leaking. All of the animals had God-given sense to go to the ark by twos. Male and female. Everything at this time was created a new. Some of the creatures weren't allowed in the ark. God covered the whole earth when he sent the flood. Can you just pause and ponder; how did the grand canyon became so awesome? A torrent of water welling up from beneath and above moving dirt, and rocks such as the Grand Canyon could have been created.

Healing in a book called "Genuine Recovery." It is very good. It goes into more detail. The words of God are telling us that faith is the substance of things hoped for; the evidence of things not seen. Through faith we understand that the worlds were framed by the words of God so that things which are seen were made of things which do not appear. This scripture is good because it tells us about faith and how real it is. It's pure logic. God knows what all things are made of. And all things are made of things that we can't see with the naked eye. There are cells finely tuned body tissue and the human body is a miracle of God's creation. Everything that was made, was made by God himself.

Also, what happened to the dinosaurs? Can you explain that? Is that in science class? The earth hadn't seen rain like this before it covered the globe. Now that's Food for thought.

Now we want to go back to Cain and Able the two first brothers, sons of Adam and Eve. Oh let's see how these two brothers got along. O K, as we know but there was a problem with their gifts to God. Cain had plants and vegetables and food for man. Able had animals and he gave first things of his stock to God for an offering. God couldn't accept Cain's plants for sacrifice. God needed an animal sacrifice. Cain became angry with Able and he slew him. Cain was guilty he expected terrible punishment from God. Cain said, "I will be a vagabond and every man who finds me will want to kill me" but the Lord set a mark upon Cain so any finding him would not kill him for if they did vengeance on him. There's would be seven fold.

But truly there is no path down life without depending on the one who made us. He allowed all things to happen to you, good or bad. But when you reach the end of something important to you like your health, or the loss of a Loved one. You can learn to pray and trust God to help you out. He can put your mind at ease. The Bible, God's word. Is the textbook for all other writing. There is also a method for healing in a book called. "Genuine Recovery." It is very good. My book is very good too. It's MIND, PAIN, FEELING, HEALING. It's a little smaller book that deals with chemical imbalances and my personal message of how I got better. I found my way with medication and Drs. And nurses and newer and more faith I ever thought I had. It goes into more detail for understanding for families of mentally ill members of the family. May God bless those who befriend those who want friends. Clergy have helped so much. Marriage counselors. There is always hope. Faith is the key to unlocking a stronghold on people. *It is the substance of things hoped for, the evidence of things not seen.* Many are broken hearted for the victims of this sickness.

It took me 30 long years to find my medicine years to know myself with prayers. I let others know how I felt and asked for their prayers. Without God there is no healing for me but I found out God is the great healer.

EVERY GOOD AND EVERY PERFECT THING COMES FROM ABOVE

PRAYER IN JESUS' NAME
When the Chaplain bowed to pray
Some didn't like it and had the nerve to say so.
When they're pressing toward the mark.
They run the race and that's no lark.
Their high calling to embark.
Holding fast to Christ the rock.
Keep on Praying for the men and women
Who are keeping our freedom from oppression
Their families so far away, How do they get
by day to day? When we kneel our prayers to
say. "Keep them Father out of harm's way."
Let them pray in Jesus's name

anonymous.

One day the helicopter that flies over our house frightened me really bad.

I never noticed it before. I was driving my old car. I just got in the driveway. I had brought two drinks and sandwiches and there right above me was this big loud helicopter. It scared me so bad that I couldn't think. I knew my car was going to overheat and blowup. I couldn't get it turned off and me in the house. I called for help again. Needed help. It stayed there and stayed there. I called out for help. I honked my horn. I needed some one to help me get into my house My new neighbor and the A/C man heard me and helped me into the house. It hoovered over me making that helicopter chopper noise over me. It was so loud I couldn't think. My neighbor heard me and He got me into the house. I have never been so frightened before or since.

Jeanie's Story

MY FAVORITE COUSIN IN MINNESOTA;

I stood before a bulletin board in a quiet hallway of my college campus in 1972. A flier on the bulletin board had caught my attention and I stopped to read it carefully.

It described a summer opportunity to teach backyard Bible Clubs in northern Indiana over the upcoming summer. The clubs were called Good News Clubs and I knew all about them because I had attended good News Clubs for several years was I was growing up. Sometimes my mother hosted the clubs at our house and one of her friends taught the lessons. It was in Good News club that I first understood that when Jesus died on the cross, He did it to take away my sin. He did it for me. He did it for everyone. I wasn't very old then but I was old enough to know that I was a sinner and needed Jesus's forgiveness.

For me, that was the beginning of a lifetime of learning about God in Heaven and his son Jesus. Twenty years after my childhood Good News Club experiences, I stood in the college hallway considering the possibility of sharing the good news of Jesus's love with children in Northern Indiana. I felt excitement bubbling up inside of me. I knew what I wanted to do that summer. I made note of the contact information, tucked away in my mind that exciting dream for my summer, and headed on to my next college class.

That evening in the dorm room, my roommate began to tell me about a job possibility for her summer. She seemed very excited as she began to tell me about it and I listened eagerly to what she had to say. How surprised and happy I was to learn that she also had read about teaching Good News Bible clubs that summer and wanted to apply!

We both applied and were accepted to serve that summer in northern Indiana with Child Evangelism Fellowship. Our assignment was to lead four backyard Good News Clubs each day for a week in one town. Then we would drive to a different town and repeat the process the next week, and would continue to do that for most of our summer.

After completing that Spring semester of college, my parents made the day long trip from Iowa to Indiana to pick me up and take me home for a couple weeks' for a couple of weeks before I had to return to Indiana. How I was going to get back to Indiana to teach Good News Clubs was still unclear, and after my parents talked it over, they felt they could not make another long trip to Indiana.

I remember that conversation with my mom. She sat down with me an explained that there would have to be some other way to get me back to Indiana. She and Dad did not know how it would work out so she said to me, "Let's just pray about it and ask for God's help." We did pray together. A few hours later, our phone rang and my mom answered it. I could hear a warm lilt in her voice, She sounded happy to be talking with someone special. I couldn't figure out who it was, probably a friend or relative she hadn't talked with in quite a while. It wasn't long until I heard my mom.

"Praise the Lord!" The phone call wasn't a very long one, so It was soon that she came to tell me that God had answered our prayer. A cousin of mine in Indiana had been given some unexpected time off from work for a few days, so he can his wife had decided to drive to Iowa for a short visit, and yes. When the timing was perfect! When their visit in Iowa came to an end, it was time for me to take my trip back to Indiana to teach Good News Bible clubs. So with suitcase in hand, I climbed into the car and rode back to Indiana with my cousins.

My mother taught me a lifetime lesson that day. She taught me to be quick to pray and quick to believe that God hears and answers our prayers. By Jeanie K.

Larry

My husband's birthday is in September this year on the 13th. this year. We just had my birthday on August 12. That was exactly one year ago that I began my second book. "Learning is Grand" It's poems and short stories for parents, teachers and kids. For grandparents too.

All of his formative years he had pain in his hips in winter. As a teen he didn't go out for sports he wanted to. I stole him right off the farm in Iowa. He was 28. I worked at his place of employment. He let J. Frances take me out first. I was too timid to take on J. Francis. He took me on his motorcycle at 80 miles per hour. I didn't feel safe.

I have such handsome, brave pictures of Larry in my mind. What a sweetheart when he was a boy. He wanted to move to Florida because his hips were hurting so bad. Then told him to wait 25 years to have his hip surgery done so they had the technology to do it right. Now he is self-confident and so practically smart. He is way past me. He is also very devoted to his church friends and he uses good judgment there.

I took him off the farm I disrupted his parents' lives. But they were pretty good to me. They came to see us in Florida a lot. They loved their granddaughter and bought her M&MS.

Larry put together and set up new machinery at International Harvester Company. He delivered farm machinery, combines, tractors, plows. And all the farm machinery. Fixed or brand new machines. eating so much, so do I. But I wish I was about 40 pounds lighter. I'm his wife.

Larry had pain in his hips all his life, Pain at birth. He had to go to the hospital once while he was young for a shot for flu. The nurse used a needle that was so long it pierced his bone. His arm was almost lost. The Doctor dug out the bad stuff and stitched him up in his left arm. To this day. It looks like a shark bit him.

Five years ago he had surgery on his hips both of them from birth. A congenital hip displacement Larry felt it was the time to do it. Since then he has adjusted to life without pain, and he is a Larry nobody knew. He's so self assured now.

He was a trouble shooter with his fellow employees there at the store. For break he would get a bottle of pop and put peanuts in it. He enjoys life basically. And he just enjoys life now, especially since he had his hip surgery.

While he had therapy at home a nice young man, his therapist came twice a week,. He taught him how to do exercises in bed. And to use pillows to give him comfort. On his feet and legs. He used a walker and then he used a cane in the house. I brought him every thing he needed. He watched T.V. and I would sew to keep busy. I think I made crochet pieces. Or worked on blankets. I sewed 5 brides maid's dresses; color, black. I guess I did O.K. I sewed pillows.

Larry took time off for his hip surgery He had good medical insurance. It certainly was worth it for his company. Now he goes to the doctor to have his chick ups and tests for his job I suppose he'll be home around is so gracious and he has the most trouble ordering his medication. His employer requests health requests.

His horse named Susie Q used to ride 6 girls on her back she was a gentle horse. Larry rode her out at his farm. He had a saddle and stirrups. He had her until I stole him away from the farm.

Wednesday, July 20, 2016 Larry told me his brothers had a Weimerwiemer dog. He put up his tail, it had been bobbed off and pointed his nose and one paw went up he was a bird dog.

Pat, the blue parakete was Larry's bird. He talked to him, made little sounds and clicked with his tongue. Pat would look up and cock his head. Pat laid a white egg. Now it was known that Pat really was Patsy. Larry left for Des Moines for trade school. Tank was a St. Bernard. A rescue dog named Tank followed Larry's dad around the farm. Dad liked him.

We had Peeky our dog. She stayed outdoors most of the time. No it is so hot we would have to let her in. It's been 90 degrees. So hot for the past two weeks. I'd have to let her in. It might be nice to have a dog companion. Just feed it twice a day. And let it out when he told me he needed to go. To the bathroom. I'd let him go outside for a little while. He could stay in and be my companion for a while ago. She was pretty redish brown dog. We have a chain link fence around the back yard. We had to have a swing set and a sand pile for our daughter to play in the back yard. I't just too hot to keep her there very long.

The Blond
by Sherri Lund

Very early in the morning while driving to my class I noticed a European sports car ahead. A man and a woman were traveling along this lonely stretch of interstate with me. Their convertible top was down and the woman's beautiful Blond hair was flying all over. She was not wearing a scarf to prevent her hair from being tangled by the 65+ mph winds surrounding the vehicle. I instantly became angry. Did the man driving not notice this passenger's rapidly whipping Hair? How was this possible? He had to have known. I thought, what a creep! Why were they riding down the road with the top down? Her hair was going to be a huge mess. "What a jerk!" I said. I just could not believe how inconsiderate this man could be to this lady.

I decided to move to the passing lane in order to see who this thoughtless man was.. I also wanted to see what Kind of woman would allow herself to be treated in such a thoughtless manner. I accelerated past the sports car. I quickly turned my head to look at this ridiculous pair. A huge burst of laughter came out of my mouth. Oh my goodness! I could not believe it. Sitting in the passenger seat next to this middle aged man was his golden retriever!

The dog was happily panting. His long blond ears flapped all over as the wind rushed over the windshield and over the passengers of the sports car. I instantly felt foolish. I had jumped to conclusions, became angry and insulted this carefree pair for the last few miles. I will never forget that lesson I learned on that early overcast morning on the interstate. Looks can be deceiving.

A Teacher in Indiana

The kids Christmas in 4th Grade, 1995. Their teacher tells of some smart alecks or according to Websters dictionary "obnoxious cleverness" put her in a chair and and tied her up there and put a Santa Hat on her then put shaving creaming on around on her face. Well they pushed her around and she sang out HO HO HO Merry Christmas! The kids loved it and the principal was in good humor too. The Teacher had her students say, "Good morning, dear principal."

He wore a Santa hat too! Teachers were doing finals for the year in Indiana. When School was out, our teacher got on the intercom and sang "Old Kentucky Home," "Go Wildcats," and "Kentucky Team!"

IT WAS A BIRTHDAY for our daughter. We ate at Joe's Crabshack. Last year they had a pony on a stick that she rode around the table a couple of times, and we sang Happy Birthday. That was neat! Pretty funny too.

I went to the Dr. for breathing and nasal problems it took me a long time to see the Dr. It was freezing in there. He said I was all fixed up. I can now. My ears don't whistle any more. I'm glad I don't have to go back to him again. It took me an extra hour to see my Doctor at ENT, ear, nose, and throat.

I guess one of the Nurses didn't come in. I looked for my driver in the cafeteria. She got some coke and took a pill didn't have any money more to buy a crush drink. And I waited and prayed God would send the Doctor in. He checked my ears, it was O.K. He checked my nose and it was O.K. I was so happy to be done there. I had done the right things. I was finished with today. I never want to go back there.

God spoke to the fathers in the past by the prophets. The old testament patriarchs of God. In these last days spoke to us by his son whom he hath appointed heirs of all things. God made the worlds. The patriarchs were looking for a city given to them by God.

Jesus who being the brightness of his glory, and the express image of his person, and upholding all things by the word of his power, when he had by himself purged our sins, sat down on the right hand of the

Majesty on High. Think about that for a while. Even the angels knew his inheritance, a more excellent name than they.

No more was blood to be shed for the offering for sin since Jesus Christ fulfilled all the sacrifices for ever and ever Moses went up to Mt. Sanai he listened to the Lord. These words the lord spoke to Moses unto all your assembly in the mount out of the midst of the fire, of the cloud, and of the thick darkness, with a great voice and he added no more. And he wrote them in two tablets of stone and delivered them to Moses. For the word of God is quick and powerful and sharper than any two edged sword. Piercing even to the dividing even of the marrow and our bones.

We must not forsake ourselves from going to church. God spoke out in the cloud, and of the thick darkness, with a great voice and he added no more as follows;

He wrote them in two tablets of stone.

Deuteronomy 5, Old Testament
TEN COMMANDMENTS

1. THOU SHALL HAVE NO OTHER GODS BEFORE ME. THOU SHALT LOVE THE LORD THY GOD.

2. THOU SHALL NOT MAKE THEE ANY GRAVEN IMAGE, OR THOU SHALL NOT BOW DOWN UNTO THEM OR SEEK THEM.

   LORD THY GOD AM A JEALOUS GOD. Visiting the iniquity of the fathers upon the Children unto the third and fourth generation of them that hate me. And showing mercy unto thousands of them that love me and keep my commandments. Thou shalt not take the name of the Lord thy God in vain for the lord will not hold him guiltless that taketh his name in vain. Keep the sabbath day to sanctify it, as the lord thy God hath commanded thee.

3. THOU SHALL NOT TAKE THE LORD'S NAME IN VAIN.

4. KEEP THE SABBATH DAY HOLY. SANCTIFY. SIX DAYS SHALL LABOR AND DO ALL THY WORK.

5. HONOR THY FATHER AND THY MOTHER. THAT THY DAYS BE PROLONGED AND THAT IT WILL BE WELL WITH THEE.

6. THOU SHALL NOT KILL.

7. NEITHER SHALL THOU COMMIT ADULTERY.

8. NEITHER SHALL THOU STEAL.

9. NEITHER SHALL THOU BEAR FALSE WITNESS AGAINST THY NEIGHBOR.

10. NEITHER SHALL THOU DESIRE THY NEIGHBOR'S WIFE NEITHER SHALL THOU COVET THY NEIGHBOR'S HOUSE. OR ANY THING THAT IS THY NEIGHBORS.

Though I speak with the tongues of men and of angels, and have not charity, I have become as sounding brass, or a tinkling cymbal. And though I have the gift of prophecy, and understand all mysteries, and all knowledge, and though I have all faith, so that I could remove mountains, and have not charity I am nothing. And though I bestow all my goods to feed the poor, and though I give my body to be burned and have not charity, it profits me nothing. Charity suffers long and is kind Charity envieth not charity vaunteth not itself is not puffed up. There is more read on….Doth not behave itself unseemly, seeketh not her own. Is not easily provoked, thinketh no evil. Rejoice not in iniquity but rejoiceth in the truth. Beareth all things believeth all things. Hopeth all things endureth all things. Charity never faileth.

I Corinthians chapter 13

I believe anyone will like this book. It has some interesting content and will lift heavy burdens off mental problems, as well as to display for all the promises God has for us.

Small Town Girl in the Big City

There are places I have been. That special people have been there for me. I was a brownie in Girl scouts. Mrs. Johnson our leader wrote to me that I was a nice girl and it was so special to me.

She reached out to me. She was so giving and pretty and her daughter Anita was a favorite class mate with pretty clothes she was a special young lady. I had the same classmates through my elementary years of school. We were the same group year after year. I was a busy youngster. I liked to succeed and I liked to win. I really had one special boy that I loved. In sixth grade. He had sandy hair. At recess playing Kick ball he jumped high right over the kick ball. He was so utterly in control and a very talented youngster. He was there for me in 6th grade.

He wrote me a note that I saved for such a long time. He sent me a card too. He wrote me that I was the prettiest girl in school. The card was a computer, before it's time. He bought me a card with this message. "they don't make them like like you." This card was a computer. They were new at that time. That was the first time I had seen a computer he was so smart and his Daddy was an attorney. They moved to a city so I had to live with that. Their family moved out of our town and away from our church. She wanted to serve her Lord; praise him. I played my trumpet for the meaning and beauty and praise to our Great God. I played for the beauty He liked the technique. That was different than mine. One day our pastor who played trumpet too had us in a trio up in front of church by the organ. After we played our special he announced I was the" rose bud" in between two thorns, What special memories

I had! I was content with my music and my Mother was right there giving me opportunities in music. I learned the music of alto from her. My dad could sing good too. He harmonized in baritone and tenor. We sang in church. What a special thing to have talented parents. There is no better music than to praise God. My Mother's special song was The Love of God how rich how pure and true. It reaches to the lowest level and the highest realm. It was something like that. Mom had a love for people and she was so engagingly in love with God She spent time on her knees praying through to him in her bedroom. She implored God's blessing on her life and her family and other people. When there was a problem or a need she prayed through to God. I wish she had shown me how to do that. She had such emotion. She showed it when her nose would get red. She knew true love.

My daughter saw me actually cry in church. I cried in Sunday school to. I was a terrible person. Always working hard and never sure of forgiveness for my sins.

She hated that. She couldn't be around me at those times. I feel so bad if I don't keep my emotions under control.

Irma Bombeck was a truly funny Christian comedian She gave her live to make people other women laugh. She took God's word to her life that laughter is the best medicine. And devoted her later years to that. I so respect her and know she is basking in heaven after doing God's good pleasure while she was on earth.

Another good mother-comedian was Barbara Jenkins. She had a practical husband who tolerated her calling to make jokes about the most terrible sins that her son did. He decided he was homosexual She wasn't brow beating him, but I would have been so ashamed I would never have been quiet about it. I would think it was my moral responsibility to reprimand my child for being homosexual. It would have been a terrible scene. In His Holy Bible God makes it clear that using your sex to guide your life in sinful ways. Just for your own pleasure. It is called a sin against your own body. It may take a lifetime to find release from that. I have that. I Know something about that.

Can you see how my daughter put up with me. She had to be some kind of perfect to be under my table. She put up with all my standards and strictness. I didn't deal with my problems until it is too late. I was prey to the opposite sex who always wanted to bother me and I didn't know how to protect myself. I was emotionally and sexually scared for life. I have wondered so many times why God puts up with me It is so hot in Florida. My nurse was so good to inspire me to write and It's pretty good. It may be a sort of legacy. I am not going to touch the air conditioner again. It gets so hot in here or so cold I can't breathe so be it. I'll not touch the air conditioner again and I will not go out side again. My brother was right I was beating a dead horse trying to be a writer and author . for dinner, finished off the salad my husband told me I could have. Now I don't have to east again at all just It should last me tonight and tomorrow. Well, the sad story is that also a I had I have an eating disorder. But it makes me a very fast typist. I shouldn't have had all of this sweet food. So high in sugars. I don't know what just comes over me. Don't know what comes over me. I have a huge eating disorder. I'll be the first to admit. I'll have to go over to my have time for beauty rests. Oh well, when I chose to do what I did. There will be circumstances. To face and I will be alone. I had some chocolate milk. That's what I needed. I have lots of energy He calls it yogurt. I call it ice cream. There won't be any for him hope I live to see another day Don't even now when I'll even get to sleep in my bed. I'm just too filled with energy from all that sweet stuff. I didn't eat those cherries. I Enough about that. I worked nights after high school I was working at Waffle House nights in Kokomo, Indiana. I was a waitress there. Mom took me to work. She worked nights at the Howard Community Hospital. She was the admissions clerk and she was smart. She went to teacher's college in Iowa and she taught in a one room school house for nine years in northern Iowa.

A man came in to the restaurant where I worked at Waffle House in Kokomo. He wanted to talk to me. I didn't know much about strangers. I didn't know how pretty I was or how to protect myself for my greatest good. I talked to him and found out he was an ex-con. He said he would buy me a car. Well, I didn't believe him. I didn't know anything about people with money. I just knew I didn't want to be used by any man who had money. I sensed how he could use me to get what he wanted. I didn't want to oblige him at all.

Another man came into Waffle House restaurant where I worked and sat on a bar stool. He talked to me about how I would never get a good reference or have a really good job like work for the government in Washington, D.C. Why would anybody, a stranger want to defeat a young lady he hardly knew. He didn't know me from "Eve". But I had no desire to do anything but talk to those creeps.. But who was this stranger anyway. He had no hold on my life. He probably had so many problems himself he just wanted to make somebody else miserable.

It is Saturday already tonight. I have to take charge of myself to make Sunday a day to remember.

I need to get my lower teeth fixed by going to the dentist. They have rotted away. Actually I had chocolate milk. When I go up to my room I will spill out. Laws of nature will prevail. We didn't have any ice cream. So I had chocolate milk. I'm not supposed to eat ice crème. It can always makes me so sick. I have somewhat of an eating disorder.

I'm not cutting my hair so short again. I'm sure my husband knows I had chocolate milk. He usually knows everything about me.

Small town, population 2500. 1963 Palm Sunday tornadoes ripped through central Indiana destroying our local high school building in Greentown. There was no school for a time. We got a new bigger school with real full size swimming pool, a new gymnasium and a new band room with risers and sound booth and plenty of storage area for the bigger musical instruments.

I had a 24 "bicycle, blue fenders, and white handle grips. I rode all around town, sidewalks, alley ways, streets; To the fairgrounds. Past some class mates houses. My brother started out riding with me but I don't know where he went.

In the summer, I had to find things to do. I went to my girl friend's house. She was a neighbor. They built a new house. I always loved new houses and wished we could have one. Our house was 100 years old. We listened to her records of the "Beatles" in her room. She had their pictures up on her walls.

I didn't know what a computer was. I took typing class and general prep courses. As a senior 97 students I was 12th in the class academically for the year. I didn't really have any friends. I just learned music, to play my trumpet and sports. I learned how to hit the tennis ball and we had a basketball hoop in our backyard. Mom was the coach of our "Pig Tails" girls softball team. We practiced at the school. I was the pitcher. Beth Bagwell pitched too. We went to play some other girl's teams were out of our league. But we had the best football team. Our farm boys gave us the best team in our range of teams and schools to make us first and best of all the other schools in football.

I took music lessons in the summer with our band director, Mr. Whorwell. He played clarinet and knew some of the other instruments. I also took piano lessons and trumpet in Kokomo. In Greentown and later on when I got older My mother drove to Indianapolis for my trumpet lessons. Mother helped me go to music camp in Cedar Lake Music Camp in Indiana for two weeks. And the following year to Pennsylvania for two weeks. I loved it so much I met a girl who impressed me. She was from Dolton Illinoise a suburb of Chicago. I only lived to go back to music camp next year. Mom made my beautiful light green graduation gown and I wore it there to play my solo.

I sold candy bars to some of the other girls in our housing. I had a fun friend, I can't believe I drove to visit her it was in Dolton Illinois. Her mother was having her kitchen remodeled so we ate supper in their basement. Her dad asked me if I wanted to pray. I prayed that if I had been in the Garden of Eden I would not have eaten of the forbidden fruit.

I went to school with my friend In her high school. There were three thousand students. I went to class with her. She took shorthand class. Her dad was driving when a policeman stopped us. He said he was driving too fast. He apologized and didn't get a ticket. His car was an old taxi cab repainted black. It had lots of room in the back seat. We went to a protest march in Chicago. I think we were protesting the war in Vietnam. We just walked with the other protesters. There was a television camera. It wasn't hostile; kind of silent. Some people had signs.

I remember the favorite scripture song, *The Lord is my light and my salvation, whom then shall I fear. The Lord is he strength of my life, of whom then shall I be afraid. Psalm 27*

Well a good thing is that I don't hear any crickets scraping this morning. I did the other morning. I was up early the other morning too. I hugged Tom after church on Sunday. He said he had my books at his desk at home too. I'm waiting to get my shot too. I guess I need it I feel O.K. today. I feel like I have 9 Lives. Too just like a cat. We don't have any grandchildren but we have grand cats; three of them. Leo, Sabrina, and Velvet. I know Marilyn's cat keeps her such good company too. We don't have a cat and it's just as well. Larry would be the one to take care of it too. I wouldn't the first thing. I missed. A man spoke to me and offered to by me a car. I already had one. He was an ex-con man.

Bibliography

The King James Bible

Recovery periodical. Magazine

Genuine Recovery By. Edward Smith

Baby Chick By Lois Lund Learning is Grand

Mind, Pain, Feeling, Healing, New Beginnings

www.thewaybooks.com

www.ingramcontent.com/pod-product-compliance
Lightning Source LLC
Chambersburg PA
CBHW031239120626
46545CB00003B/1193